To my two greatest gifts.

You inspire me with your creativity,

your joy, your eternal optimism,

and your unconditional love.

You make the world a better place.

May you always see a rainbow view.

Limitless Little Leaders Series
Lovey Livy Lu: A Rainbow View

ISBN: 978-0-578-94962-8 (hardcover)

Published by elivate

First printing edition 2022

For more information, teaching tools, activities, and other resources, visit
www.gialacqua.com

LOVEY Livy LU

a Rainbow View

written by GIA LACQUA
illustrated by ZUZANA SVOBODOVÁ

Hi! Nice to meet you! I'm Livy Lu.
I LOVE rainbows - from the red to the blue.

After the rain, I look for rays of light.
Up in the sky, it's a beautiful sight.

Mommy?
Layla said something
that made me think -
That in all the rainbow's colors,
there is no pink!

Is that true, Mommy? Is what she said right?

Because *you* told me rainbows are a range of light.

That's true, rainbows show all their colors in the sky.

Then why would Layla tell me a lie?

Layla said what she believes is true.

Sometimes it just depends on your view.

She was picturing a rainbow on paper,
You were imagining a real rainbow, in nature.

There are seven colors at the very first glance, but lots of shades in between

... if you give it a chance!

What do you see when
the sun peeks out
of the skies?

A beautiful sunset?

An early sunrise!

Our class saw a chameleon
when we went to the zoo.

I thought
he was green...

...but Jake said blue.

Exactly! That cloud up there
looks just like a house.

That's not a house!

It's a teeny, tiny mouse.

Everyone's view is based on what they see.

It's fun to think about all the possibilities!

There's more than one way to look at a riddle.

This way, or that way...

... or somewhere in the middle.

That's why we must remember
to keep an open mind.
Ask questions, stay curious,
and always be kind.

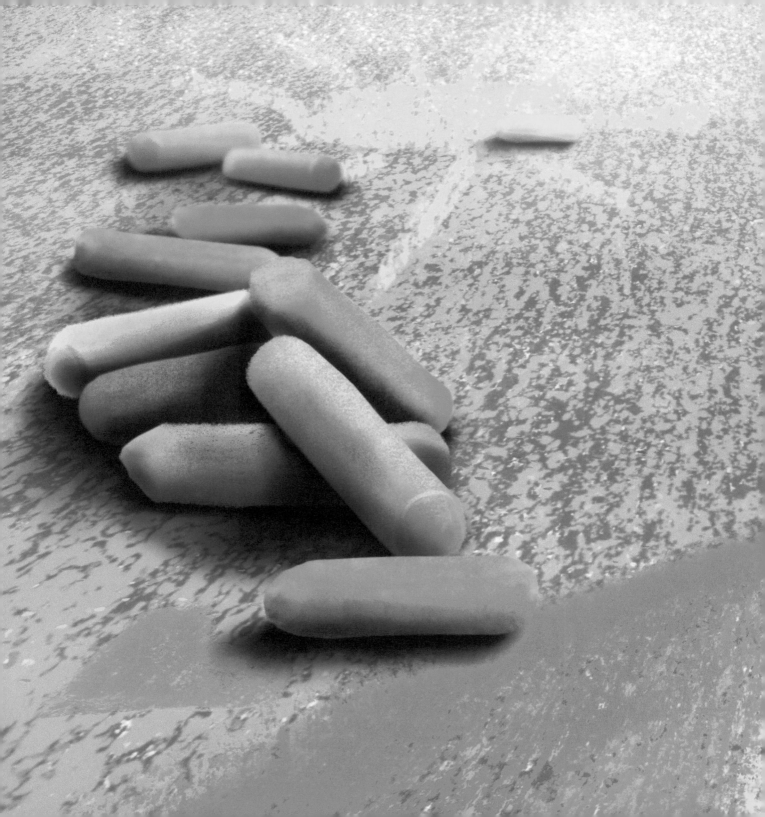

So Layla wasn't wrong

when she said there's no pink.

It just depends on how you think!

Sometimes we need to question things we thought we knew. Because you might just see another point of view.

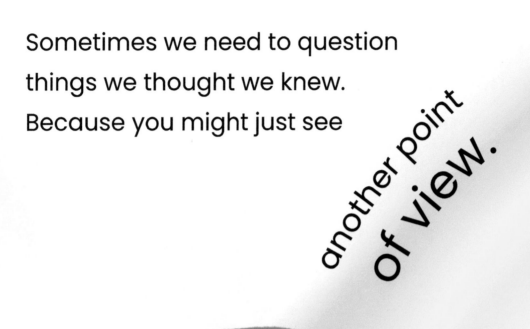

ABOUT
the author

GIA LACQUA is a children's book author, proud mom of two girls, successful former business executive, Certified Professional Coach, entrepreneur, and Founder & CEO of elivate, a boutique empowerment coaching firm based in the New York City area. Raised in northern New Jersey, Gia earned her Bachelor of Science in Human Development from the University of Connecticut and serves as board member with the Girl Scouts of Northern New Jersey.

Whether she is working with future leaders in kindergarten classrooms or current leaders in boardrooms, Gia is fueled by her passion for helping others grow through change.

elivate

AUTHOR
letter

DEAR PARENTS, CAREGIVERS, AND EDUCATORS,

The Limitless Little Leaders picture book series is designed to teach children lifelong empowerment and mindset skills that will set them up for a lifetime of happiness and success, no matter what life throws their way.

For more information on the Limitless Little Leaders series, teaching tools, activities, and other resources, visit **www.gialacqua.com**.

For more information on empowerment coaching, visit **www.theelivategroup.com**.

If you have any questions about the book series, classroom empowerment activities and lessons, and/or empowerment coaching, please contact me at **gia@gialacqua.com**.

Thank you for joining me on this important mission to educate, inspire, and empower our limitless little leaders.

Your partner in success,
Gia

@gialacqua
#limitlesslittleleaders

CPSIA information can be obtained
at www.ICGtesting.com
Printed in the USA
BVHW021508030322
630566BV00007B/231